CW01651159

A Day Out

Teachers' Book

INCLUSIVE READERS SERIES

A Day Out

Teachers' Book

Maggie Walker
Val Davis
Ann Berger

David Fulton Publishers
London

David Fulton Publishers Ltd
Ormond House
26–27 Boswell Street
London WC1N 3JZ

First published in Great Britain in 2002 by David Fulton Publishers Ltd

British Library Cataloguing in Publication Data
A catalogue record is available from the British Library.

ISBN: 1-85346-925-4

Designed and typeset by Kenneth Burnley, Wirral, Cheshire
Photographs by John Redman; illustrations on pages 43, 44, 47 by Caroline Burnley
Printed and bound in Great Britain by Bell and Bain Ltd, Glasgow

Contents

Note: All of these resources may be photocopied, cut out and laminated as required.

Introduction

Pupils who are at the early stages of acquiring literacy skills need motivating texts to support their learning. The Inclusive Readers series of books is designed to provide this. It is based on the scheme of work developed by Bristol Schools, which has been published in the second edition of *Implementing the Literacy Hour for Pupils with Learning Difficulties* (David Fulton 2001).

The big books include fiction, non-fiction styles and poetry, and each individual book focuses on one specific genre that should be covered in Key Stage 2. Some of the texts are also suitable for use with pupils in Years 7 and 8. In the centre of each big book is a pull-out section, which features characters and objects from the texts that can be cut out and laminated, and used to support multisensory teaching strategies. Each Teachers' Book includes a wide range of activities that can be used with pupils to reinforce their understanding of the text and the development of word and sentence level skills. They are linked to the Key Stage 1 objectives in the National Literacy Strategy but designed to be appropriate for pupils between 7 and 12 years of age.

The Teachers' Book also includes three differentiated texts based on the big book, which are designed to be used during guided reading work. They are produced at three levels linked to the revised P scales. The P5–P6 and P7–1C books have symbols as well as words to reinforce reading skills. The level 1B–2C books have only words. Each of these differentiated texts is illustrated with black and white versions of the pictures from the big book, and is fully photocopiable for individual use, and also for the use of parents to support pupils at home.

We have worked closely with Widgit Software to develop appropriate symbols for certain key words. These symbols can be copied and used in other contexts to reinforce the learning. They are also available for Writing with Symbols.

This text is based on a visit by a Y4 class from New Fosseway Special School in Bristol to the arboretum near Tetbury in Gloucestershire. The class consists of all boys, and not all of them are shown in the photographs. The visit took place on a beautiful October day, although underfoot it was still wet from recent rain. As well as hundreds of trees, the arboretum has wide open spaces, and most of the children loved just running and chasing the brilliant-coloured leaves. There were lots of schoolchildren visiting the arboretum that day, in their uniforms with their clipboards and worksheets, but none of them displayed the absolute joyfulness of the children from New Fosseway.

National Literacy Strategy

Weekly Plan

Class ________________ Teacher __________________________ Date ___________________

	Whole class shared reading and writing	Whole class phonics, spelling, vocabulary and grammar	Guided group tasks P1–P2	Guided group tasks P3–P4	Plenary
Mon	A DAY OUT	Make up a rap about trees. Record and use in Literacy Hour	Look at some trees from different angles – beside, under, far away, close up	Adult draws trees. Pupils draw rain, snow, sun, wind over the pictures	How do pupils respond to trees?
Tues		Visit an arboretum (or wood/forest/ group of trees, or even a single one)	Collect leaves to feel, crunch, tear, blow, wave	Make a collage of leaves	Which senses do pupils favour?
Wed	Look at pictures or photographs of trees in different seasons		Put lots of leaves inside different kinds of containers for pupils to feel, e.g. plastic carriers, paper bags, baskets, boxes, envelopes	Make leaf prints	How do pupils respond to different touches?
Thur		Collect tree parts. Use the names as you investigate them: leaves, branches, twigs, cones, bark, berries	Hang objects from trees, e.g. paper mobiles, strips of fabric, plastic and wooden objects. Watch them move in the breeze	Paint twigs. Hang them from the ceiling. Add objects. These make good decorations if it's festival time	Do pupils look up at objects? Look down? Follow a moving object?
Fri	Depending on the season, look at fallen leaves, acorns and cones, Christmas trees, berries, blossom or big leaves		Investigate the shadows that trees form. Feel the difference in temperature and light quality. Watch moving shadows as branches and leaves blow in the wind	Pupils paint big green and brown patches. Adults put them together to form trees or even a forest!	Can pupils manipulate objects?

National Literacy Strategy

Weekly Plan

Class _______________ Teacher _______________________ Date _________________

	Whole class shared reading and writing	Whole class phonics, spelling, vocabulary and grammar	Guided group tasks P5–P6	Guided group tasks P7–P8	Plenary
Mon	A DAY OUT	Look up the word 'arboretum' in a dictionary. Have you an arboretum or something like it near your school?	Make pairs of shoes and boots from a muddled pile	Make a list of all the children in the story. Make a list of the children in your class. Do any have the same names?	Can pupils use a dictionary?
Tues	Learn some vocabulary about trees, e.g. leaves, twigs, branches, bark, roots		Draw a tree and write some of the words you know about trees	Draw a tree and label it	How many new words have pupils learned?
Wed		Visit a local arboretum, park, forest or other place with trees	Draw a picture of something you saw on your visit	Draw a picture of something you saw on your visit. Write a caption for it	Can pupils make representational drawings?
Thur	Make a list of pupils' favourite words from the story		Think about your visit and write a sentence that begins: 'I liked . . .'	Write all the words that describe the mud in the story. Can you think of any more?	Can pupils use descriptive words?
Fri		Sequence the order of things to do when you get into the minibus	Make a group book about your class visit	Talk about the beginning, middle and end of the book. Choose a sentence from each part of the book and copy it	Can pupils sequence: three events? four events? five events?

National Literacy Strategy

Weekly Plan

Class ______________ Teacher ______________________ Date ________________

	Whole class shared reading and writing	**Whole class phonics, spelling, vocabulary and grammar**	**Guided group tasks 1C–1B**	**Guided group tasks 1A–2C**	**Plenary**
Mon	A DAY OUT	Make a list of some adjectives from the book. Discuss which are most descriptive	Choose a few adjectives from the book and write another one which is similar but not exactly the same	Copy some sentences and change the adjectives to something more suitable or descriptive	Can pupils use adjectives effectively?
Tues	Discuss the use of speech marks		Copy a few sentences from the book which have speech marks	Add the speech marks to some sentences	Do pupils understand speech marks? Can they use them?
Wed		Find out why wellington boots are so called. Go to the library or ask another adult	Make a list of things you might take with you on a visit to the arboretum	Make a concertina book using pictures or photos from a class visit of the past	Can pupils find out information from a variety of sources?
Thur	Discuss the gentle humour in the book		Choose one of the characters in the book and write everything you know about him/her.	Write about your favourite class visit	Can pupils construct sentences?
Fri	Why does the author use capital letters for some words? e.g. YES, BRILLIANT, THE MUD		Match lower-case and upper-case letters. Write some words using both kinds of letters	Write some sentences that have some words in capital letters. Read them to your teacher or a friend	Can pupils write lower-case and upper-case letters? All? Some? Which?

National Literacy Strategy

Suggestions for further activities

Text: *A Day Out*

P1–P2

- Feel the bark on trees
- Put boots on pupils' feet. If they are ambulant, let them stomp around for a while
- Free play with mud – outside or inside
- An adult hides with one of the pupils. The other pupils and adults look for him/her
- Play 'What's in the bag?' games

P3–P4

- Make mud. (Use sand and water if you can't bear the mess!)
- Play hide and seek
- Make a packed lunch to share in the classroom or have a picnic
- Choose the right clothes for the weather, e.g. boots and coats on wet days; sunglasses and shorts on sunny days
- Take photos of your minibus from different angles for a display in the classroom. Highlight details of lights, steering wheel, seats, seatbelts etc.

P5–P6

- Draw a packed lunch or cut out pictures and stick them onto a picture of a lunch box
- Play Kim's Game
- Make a survey of who in your school can drive
- Draw a picture as if you were looking out of the minibus window. Label the things you can see
- Go to a tree and position the pupils so you can discuss prepositions: by, beside, next to, near, on, over, under, between

P7–P8

- Draw a picture of a packed lunch and label it
- Talk about why we need to wear seatbelts when we travel
- Learn left and right
- In the story, catching leaves brings good luck. What other things are supposed to be lucky?
- The leaves at the arboretum were all shades of autumn colours. Draw around some leaves and use these colours to make them look real

1C–1B

- Talk about why the children laughed when they got excited. What things do people do when they are sad, happy, upset, angry, afraid?
- The mud was 'squashy and squelchy'. How many more words can you find that begin with 'sq'?
- Make up a new title for this story
- Discuss the 'blurb' on the back of the book. Does it give a good account of the story?
- Talk about fiction and non-fiction. What kind of book is this?

1A–2C

- Talk about the sequence of the day's visit. Make a sequence of the things that happen on an ordinary school day.
- In the story everyone else was having 'an ordinary day'. Imagine something amazing happens on the ordinary day and tell someone about it.
- This book has photographs instead of an artist's drawings. Is it more effective? Look at several books and compare the different types of illustrations. Which do you like best?
- Imagine you could interview the children in the story about their visit. Make up a list of questions you would ask.
- Think up as many words as you can to describe one or more of the following: trees, mud, autumn, rain, fun

Multisensory pack

Wellington boots

Selection of bags and other containers

Mud or sand, and water

Leaves

Twigs

Pine cones

Acorns

Conkers

Pieces of bark

Seeds

Berries

Symbols

bus

boots

trees

leaves

mud

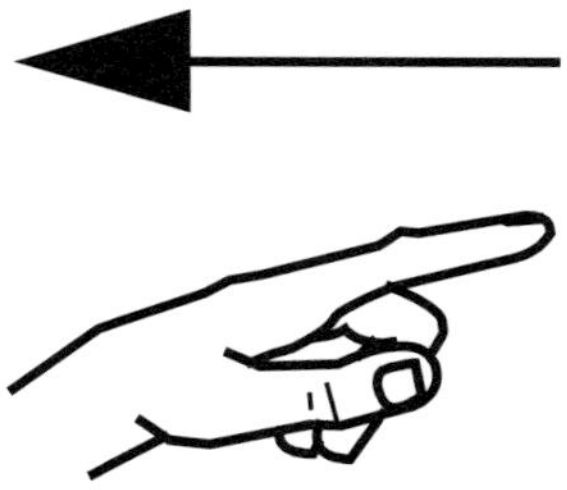

went

bags

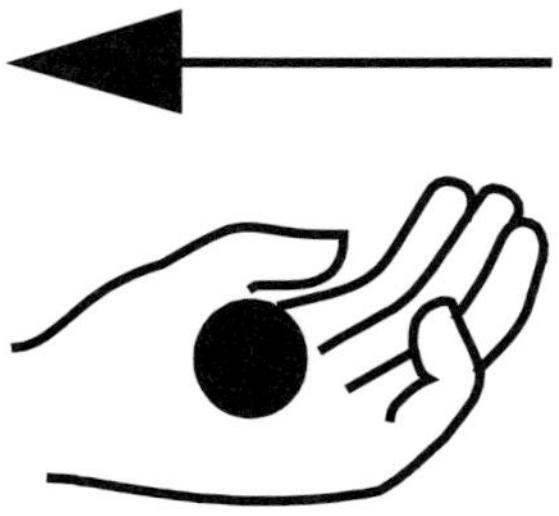

had

Symbols

we

good

saw

fun

liked

brilliant

see

Word strips

List 1

we	went
in	the
like(d)	and
on	to
see	it
was	go
at	I'm
said	play(ed)
they	

Word strips

List 2

saw	back
had	our
good	got
green	they
after	school

Word strips

Context words and name

bus	leaves
trees	mud
boots	bags
fun	brilliant
minibus	children
hungry	arboretum
splosh	yum
lunch	Michael

Differentiated versions of the text

On the following pages you will find three differentiated versions of the story *A Day Out*, for use with individual pupils working at the following levels:

The version for pupils working at levels P5–6 uses the following key words:

HF words List 1	we went in the like(d)
List 2	saw
Context words	bus trees leaves mud

The version for pupils working at levels P7–1C uses the following key words:

HF words List 1	we and went on the to see it was in
List 2	had our good
Context words	boots bags bus trees fun leaves mud brilliant

The version for pupils working at levels 1B–2C uses the following key words:

HF words List 1	at the in to go I'm said play(ed) was they
List 2	got green after had back school good
Context words	children minibus arboretum hungry trees leaves mud splosh lunch yum
Name	Michael

Each of these texts can be photocopied and made into individual books. We have also included a black and white version of the cover of the story book which can be copied, laminated and used for individual book covers.

inclusive readers

A Day Out

Maggie Walker

Photographs by John Redman

Text for pupils working at levels P5–P6

We went in the bus.

We saw the trees.

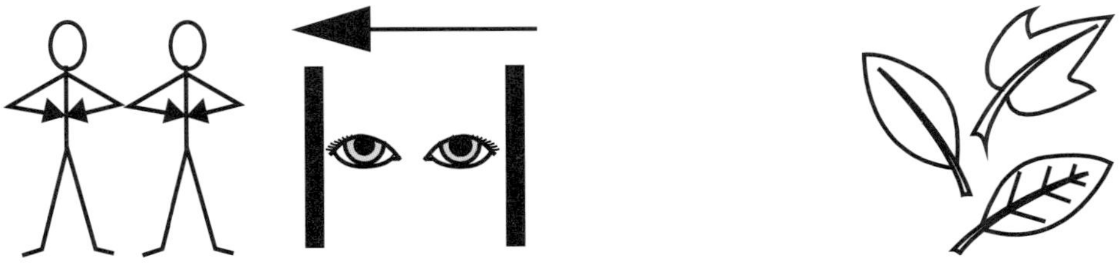

We saw the leaves.

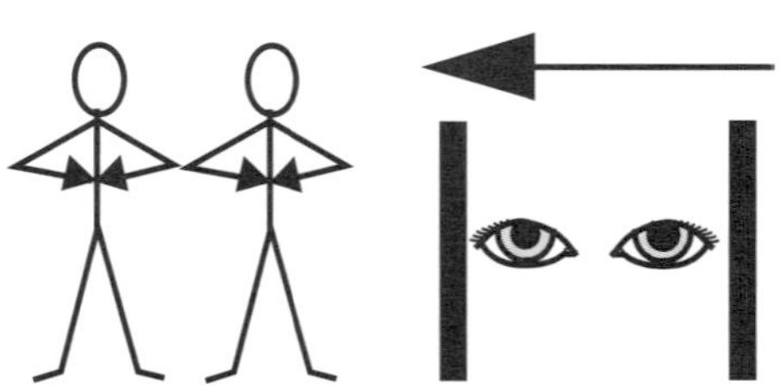

We saw the MUD.

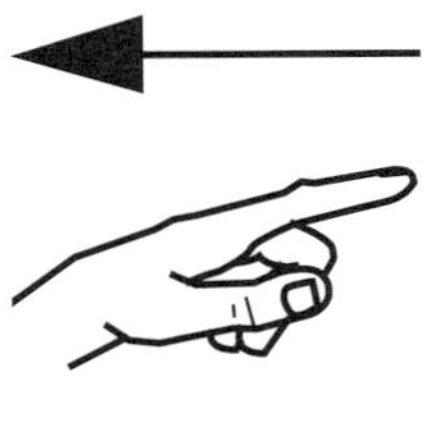

We went in the MUD.

We liked the trees.

We liked the leaves.

We liked the MUD!

inclusive ir readers

A Day Out

Maggie Walker

Photographs by John Redman

Text for pupils working at levels P7–1C

We had our boots . . .

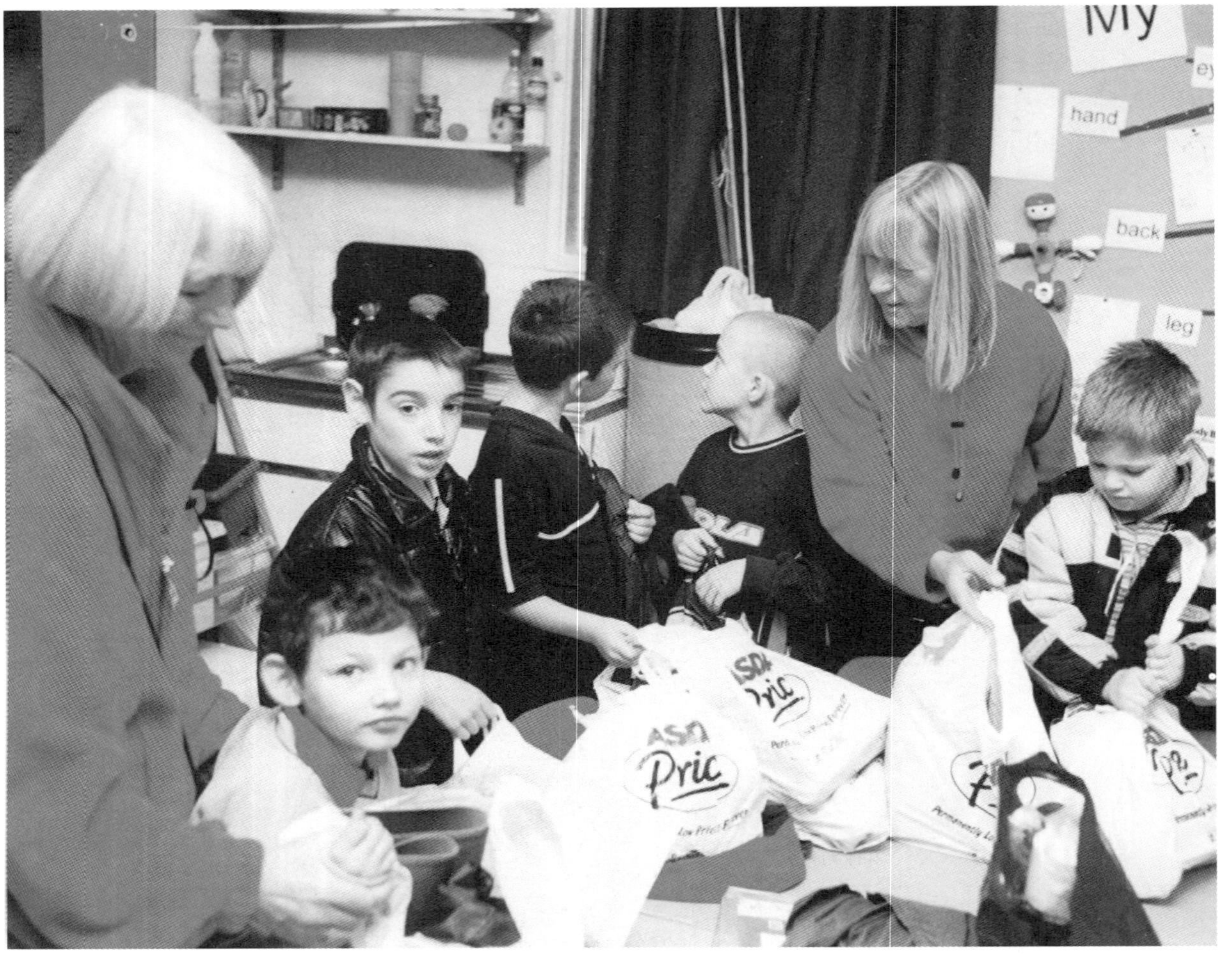

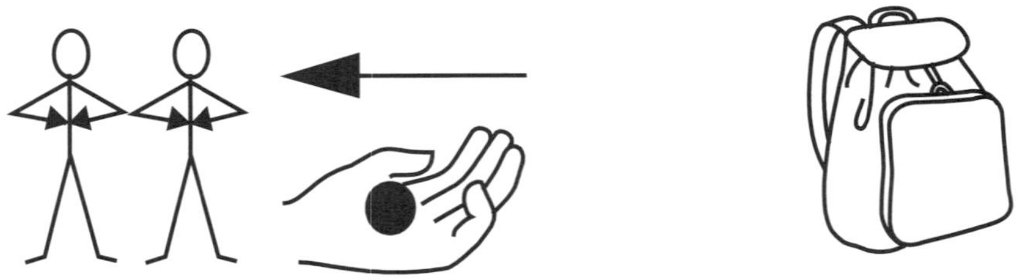

and we had our bags.

We went on the bus . . .

to see the trees.

It was good fun

on the bus.

It was good fun

in the trees.

It was good fun

in the leaves.

Text for pupils working at levels 1B–2C

At 9 a.m. the children got in the green minibus to go to the arboretum.
'I'm hungry,' said Michael.

At 10 a.m. the children played in the trees. 'I'm hungry,' said Michael.

At 11 a.m. the children played in the leaves. 'I'm hungry,' said Michael.

At 12 noon the children played in the mud. 'Splosh, splosh, splosh,' said Michael.

After the mud the children had lunch.
'Yum, yum, yum,' said Michael.

At 1 p.m. the children got in the green minibus to go back to school.

'The mud was good,' they said.

'The LUNCH was good,' said Michael.

Trees

RESOURCE SHEET 1

Name ____

Some of the tree trunks and some of the tree tops are missing. Finish the pictures.

Boots

RESOURCE SHEET 2

Name ____

Draw lines to join the matching boots together.

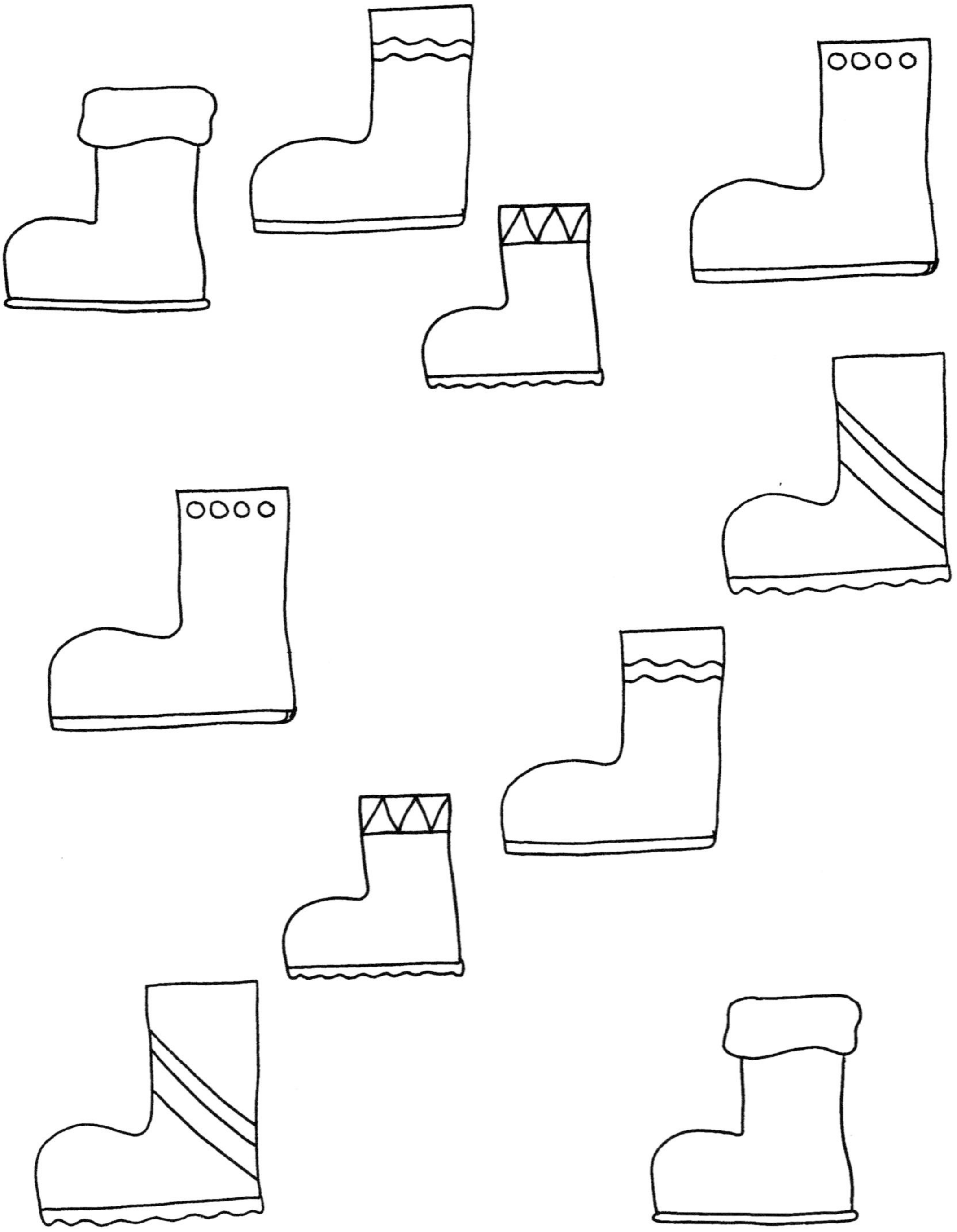

Tree raps

RESOURCE SHEET 3

Name ______________________________

Blow wind blow
Through the trees.
We can whistle
Just like you.

What shall we find in the forest?
Are there bears or wolves?
I'm feeling scared in the forest
I wish I were back home.

What shall we find in the forest?
Are there spirits or ghosts?
What's that there?! Oh No!
OK, it's just . . .

Come with me to the forest
In, in, in to the trees.
Up, up, up through the branches
Down, down, back to the ground.

Going out in the minibus

RESOURCE SHEET 4

Name ______________________________

This is a list of what you must do when you go out in the minibus. Cut the sentences out and then stick them on another piece of paper in the right order.

Fasten your seatbelt

Open the door

Sit on your seat

Get on the bus

Pick up your bag

In my lunchbox

RESOURCE SHEET 5

Name

Colour in all the things you would put in a lunchbox. Write the names underneath.

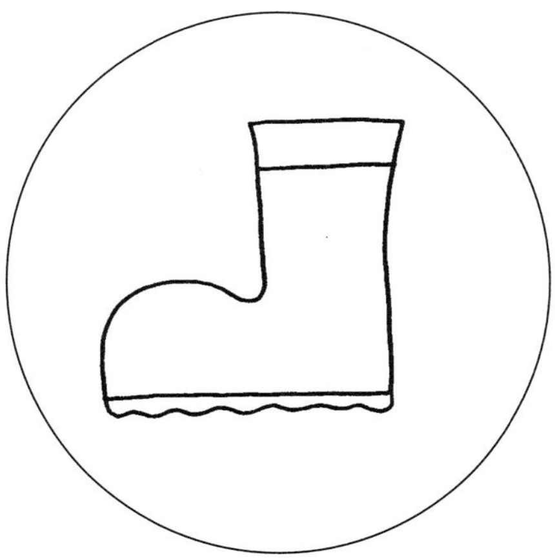

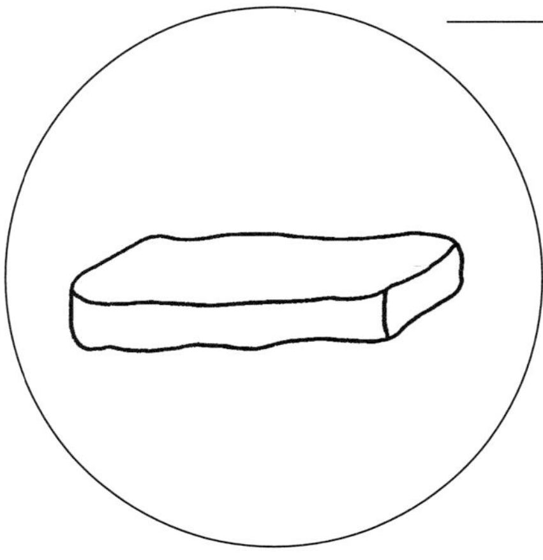

Negative sentences

RESOURCE SHEET 6

Name ____

Rewrite these sentences so they are negative. The first one is done for you.

'I like mud.'
'I don't like mud.'

'You can eat it.'

'We could eat more.'

'It is time for lunch.'

What do you notice about each pair of sentences?

Adjectives

RESOURCE SHEET 7

Name ________________________________

Change each adjective for another, more interesting word.

1. Look at the [soft] mud.

[ ]

2. I like the [big] trees.

[ ]

3. The minibus is [nice.]

[ ]

4. Here are some [good] leaves.

[ ]

Punctuation

RESOURCE SHEET 8

Name ______________________________

Punctuate these sentences with speech marks:

1. I don't like mud, said Andrew.
2. You can't eat it yet.
3. Is it time for lunch yet? said Michael.
4. Are your seatbelts on? she said.
5. Why do I have to wear boots? he said.
6. Hooray, said Anne, you're all on.
7. Your leaf is bigger than your head, said Andrew.
8. It's nearly lunchtime, Anne said.
9. It's brilliant, Andrew thought.
10. Are you ready? she called. Yes, we all said.

Verbs and pronouns

RESOURCE SHEET 9

Name ____

Write the correct verb in each space to match the pronouns.

1. I am playing.

   The children ____________ playing.

2. He is writing.

   They ____________ writing.

3. The cat ____________ sleeping.

   The cats are sleeping.

4. She is cooking.

   These men ____________ cooking.

5. I ____________ singing.

   The girls are singing.

Andrew's day out

RESOURCE SHEET 10

Name ____

Write what Andrew is saying about the mud.